Collecting and Polishing Stones

Collecting and Polishing Stones

Herbert Scarfe

B. T. BATSFORD LIMITED

© Herbert Scarfe 1970

First published 1970

7134 2283 1

Filmset by Keyspools Limited, Golborne, Lancashire

Printed and bound in Denmark by F. E. Bording Limited, Copenhagen
for the publishers B. T. Batsford Limited
4 Fitzhardinge Street, Portman Square, London W1

Contents

Acknowledgment

I wish to express my gratitude to friends and colleagues for advice and encouragement during the preparation of this book. Special thanks are due to my wife, Doreen, for valuable assistance with research; also to the members of Lapidary Societies in Scotland and England who have kindly supplied information on locations for collecting stones; and to Elizabeth Ann Fenton who designed and made the examples of jewellery.

Photographs of manufactured machines are included by courtesy of Gemstones, Hull, and the photographs (figures 30, 31, 39, 42, 44, 45) are the work of Mr Eric Johnson. Colour transparencies and additional photography by City Engraving Co. Ltd, Hull.

Kingston upon Hull 1970   H.S.

Introduction

Almost everyone, at some time or another, has picked up a pebble on the beach and wished they could preserve the attractive colour which it has when wet. Some people collect rocks from different places as souvenirs of their visits or as geological specimens. There are many stones to be found which can be termed 'semi-precious' and are worth cutting for setting into jewellery. Whatever the reason for collecting, polishing the stones will enhance their beauty, and the following chapters are intended as a guide for the beginner.

While it is not essential to have a knowledge of geology to make a collection of stones for polishing, the enthusiastic collector will inevitably wish to know more about the different types of rocks and their formation. As there are many books on geology available for study, only a brief classification and description of stones suitable for polishing is included here to assist in identification.

Although the art of stone polishing known as lapidary is an ancient craft, it is only in recent years that it has become popular as a hobby. Groups of people have formed lapidary clubs which have their own workshops where members can practise the craft. In some towns there are evening classes run by local authorities, where instruction is given in cutting and polishing stones. It has also been introduced as a craft subject in a few schools.

The methods of cutting and polishing outlined in this book have been successfully used by children and adults but, as with any craft, techniques vary with individual craftsmen and the beginner is encouraged to find the most satisfactory personal approach.

The nature of rocks and minerals

One of the difficulties which arises for the beginner is how to recognise the sort of rocks which will polish successfully, and so avoid carrying home a heavy load of unsuitable material. In order to understand the nature and origins of stones and pebbles selected for polishing, it is useful to have some idea of the structure and formation of rocks and minerals, and a brief outline is given here of some of the relevant aspects of the subject to assist identification. It is hoped that the reader will be encouraged to undertake further research into the complexities of geological science, and a list of books for general study has been appended.

Rocks are classified under three principal groups:

Igneous rocks were formed by the solidifying of molten material, known as *magma*, which was either forced up through the earth's crust by volcanic action and cooled rapidly, or welled-up under the surface where it cooled slowly as coarse-grained crystalline rocks, of which granite is an easily recognised example. Lava which cooled too quickly to crystallise properly, formed obsidian (volcanic glass) or basalt, a dark compact, very hard rock.

Sedimentary rocks consist of accumulated deposits from rock fragments in the form of sand and mud or decayed marine and vegetable matter, usually laid down in water. Consolidation of successive sedimentary layers was due to extreme pressure and some of the rocks formed in this way are chalk, limestone, sandstone and shale. It is possible for geologists to determine the age of sedimentary rocks by identification of fossil remains of past life which they contain.

Metamorphic rocks are those which have been altered from their original nature by such forces as heat and pressure. A further upsurge of molten magma melted the igneous and sedimentary rocks it contacted and re-crystallisation occurred during the slow cooling process. A similar reconstitution of existing rock was brought about by the build-up of layers of sedimentary rock causing extreme pressure, which, in turn, created enough heat to disturb the earth's crust. Limestone changed into marble, and sandstone which has become quartzite, are examples of metamorphism.

The distinction often made between rocks and minerals can be confusing, as rocks are variable compounds of different minerals. The minerals in granite, which are quartz, feldspar and mica, can easily be seen as sparkling grains and flakes but in many rocks the minerals are not visible to the unaided eye.

Rock-forming minerals are composed, in varying combinations, from natural elements such as aluminium, calcium, iron, magnesium, oxygen, potassium, silicon, and sodium. Quartz, the most common mineral, combines silicon and oxygen. The substance of any mineral has a definite chemical composition, sometimes of great complexity due to the fusion of many elements, and also possesses distinctive physical properties such as shape, cleavage, weight and hardness.

The shape assumed by a mineral is determined by the regular internal arrangement of the atoms peculiar to that mineral, and if growth conditions are suitable it will form crystals of characteristic geometric shape. The atomic structure also influences the direction of cleavage along distinctive planes of weakness. In some minerals, quartz being a good example, the atomic bond is equally strong in all directions, eliminating planes of cleavage. Cohesion, or bonding, of the structural atoms is also responsible for degrees of hardness. Hardness refers to degree of abrasive resistance but many of the softer rocks are extremely tough, with a high breaking point.

For comparison of hardness in minerals, the accepted standards are based on a scale designed by Friedrich Mohs, a German mineralogist. Although Mohs' scale provides a convenient form of reference, the numerical progression from 1 to 10 merely indicates relative stages of hardness and in no way represents the degrees of hardness between one mineral and another, for instance, the intervals of hardness between talc, gypsum and calcite are much closer than those between topaz, corundum and diamond.

Mohs' Scale of Hardness

1	Talc (softest)	6	Orthoclase
2	Gypsum	7	Quartz
3	Calcite	8	Topaz
4	Fluorite	9	Corundum
5	Apatite	10	Diamond

A simple scratch test will sometimes help to identify a specimen, and minerals can be tested against each other to determine their relative position in the scale. Other comparisons can be used as rough indications of hardness when testing minerals in the field, such as:

A fingernail, hardness $2\frac{1}{2}$, will scratch gypsum and talc.

A copper coin, hardness 4, will scratch calcite.

A penknife blade, hardness $5\frac{1}{2}$, will scratch minerals below hardness 6.

A steel file, hardness $6\frac{1}{2}$, will mark orthoclase but not quartz.

Metallic minerals such as lead (galena) and iron (haematite) can be detected by their excessive weight when compared with other mineral samples of the same size. More accurate calculations of weight are made by measuring the specific gravity, that is the weight of a mineral compared to the weight of an equal volume of water.

Some minerals have a distinctive streak, which is the colour produced when they are crushed or powdered, and this can be quite different from the surface colour. In some cases the streak can be determined by drawing the mineral across the back of a wall-tile.

Another means of identification is the lustre, or the appearance of a mineral under normal light conditions, and some of the terms used to describe this are: adamantine (brilliant as a diamond), metallic, vitreous (glassy), waxy, pearly, silky.

A combination of all these methods of determining the properties of a mineral can be used to aid identification when compared with the lists of hardness, specific gravity and other distinctive features of minerals which can be found in books dealing with mineralogy.

Stones suitable for polishing

What to look for

Stones selected purely on surface appearance, without concern for type or mineral content, can often be very rewarding when cut and polished, and common pebbles of attractive appearance should not be entirely overlooked when searching for the more rare semi-precious varieties. Most compact stones will take some degree of polish, the exceptions being certain granular and flaky varieties, which disintegrate during shaping, and stones of porous character. In knowing what to look for when selecting stones for polishing, it is equally important to know which stones to reject. In this category are included the following stones which are unsuitable for polishing, some of which are illustrated in figure 1.

Schists Highly compressed metamorphic rock, characterised by parallel layers which split easily into thin flakes. There are many varieties of schist, with fine to coarse texture, which are known by their predominant mineral constituent, such as mica-schist, quartz-schist, chlorite-schist, hornblende-schist. Some mica schists contain crystals of garnet.

Sandstone Mainly composed of minute quartz crystals. Can be finely textured or coarse-grained. Crumbles easily and is very porous. Stained by mineral oxides, green, red, brown or yellow.

Mudstone and shale Compressed clay rocks, originally deposited as clay under water and later subjected to pressure. Mineral structure microscopic. Shale has close bedding planes in parallel layers, while mudstone is more compact, smooth and finely textured.

Chalk Very soft, fine-grained limestone deposits from calcareous debris, including shell fragments and marine organisms.

Quartz-veined sandstone Veins of yellow or white quartz or red jasper variety in a groundmass of different coloured sandstone. Close inspection will show the softer sandstone area to be slightly concave, with the harder quartz veins forming a raised network.

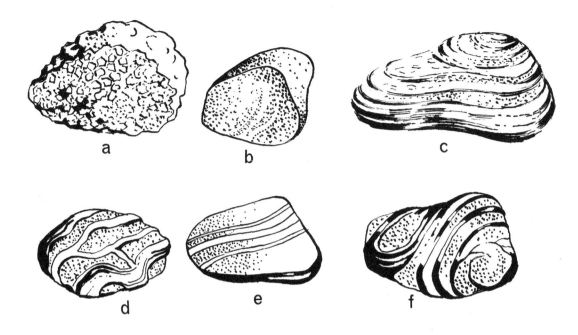

1 Stones unsuitable for polishing
Top Porous and granular varieties **a, b** Coarse and finely textured sandstones **c** Schist, composed of sandstone layers, sometimes containing silvery flakes of mica
Bottom Veined pebbles of hard and soft material **d, e** Hard quartz veins in sandstone and slate **f** Veins of red jasper in pebble of red sandstone

Quartz gemstones

A large proportion of stones and pebbles from British sources are composed of quartz in one form or another, some being of gemstone quality and, because it comes high on the hardness scale, provides some of the best polishing material.

During the formation of the igneous rocks, any surplus of silicon in the rock-forming magma became quartz, the purest variety being pure rock crystal. There are many different forms of quartz and these are classified in two groups, *crystalline*, possessing a positive internal molecular structure, and *cryptocrystalline*, which has no apparent structural form. The differences being caused by the conditions under which the silicon was deposited and variations in the rate of cooling.

Crystalline quartz Molten silicon flowing into fissures and rock cavities, cooled slowly and crystallised into the structural habit of the mineral. Well-formed quartz crystals show a distinctive hexagonal section. Groups of perfectly formed crystals of varying size developed when there was adequate space for growth and the slow rate of cooling was favourable. (Figure 2a.) Another form of crystalline quartz is known as *massive*. Subjected to the same long period

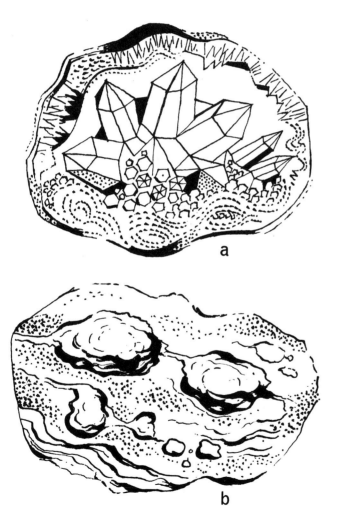

a

b

2 Formation of crystalline and cryptocrystalline quartz
a Crystalline. Section through geode showing crystal development
b Cryptocrystalline. Section through volcanic rock showing nodules and veins formed by silica streams

3 a Volcanic rock showing exposed nodules of agate and clear chalcedony
b Irregularity of shape and pitted surface of chalcedony varieties often aids identification

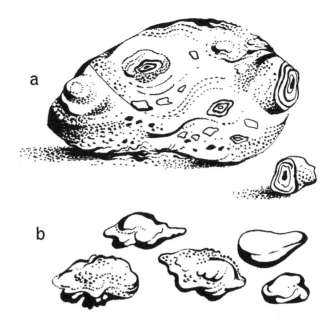

a

b

of cooling but having insufficient space for crystal growth, a tightly packed mass with the same internal molecular structure was produced.

In addition to clear rock crystal, there are several colour variations in quartz, such as purple (amethyst), yellow (citrine), and smoky brown (cairngorm), and flawless crystals of these are cut and polished as gemstones.

Cryptocrystalline quartz In this group, streams of silicon were deposited into steam ducts and gas cavities in the volcanic rock, and cooled quickly as veins and nodules. (Figure 2b.) Rapid cooling prevented crystallisation but, although not apparent, a minute fibrous structure is present in the solidified mass. The veins and nodules can be of colourless silica or fused with impurities and stained with mineral oxides. These form the chalcedony, agate and jasper varieties of quartz, which are recognised by their waxy lustre, irregular form and pitted surface.

Chalcedony and agate nodules are found embedded in volcanic rock (figure 3) in rounded form up to 3 or 4 in (76 or 101 mm) in diameter (larger nodules are rare in Britain), or in smaller almond-shaped cavities (amygdales). These are often released from the matrix by weathering and transported to beaches or other locations through the agencies of streams or boulder clay deposited by glacial action.

Removal of nodules from the rock must be carried out with care, as any direct hammering on the specimen will result in shattered fragments. A small chisel, hammered gently into the rock surrounding the nodule will eventually dislodge the specimen. When found on beaches, the chalcedony varieties of quartz are usually small, and in many cases fragmentary, due to years of movement and wear, but pieces large enough to cut and polish as gemstones are often found. The red (carnelian) variety stands out clearly among other beach pebbles but are sometimes confused with iron-stained pebbles of crystalline quartz. They are easy to differentiate when dry because quartz has a dull surface compared to the waxy appearance of chalcedony.

Classification of stones suitable for polishing from British locations

The hardness number refers to approximate position on Mohs' scale

QUARTZ *(crystalline varieties)*

Hardness: 7. Found as crystals in geodes or rock cavities, also in massive form. Found as water-worn pebbles on beaches or in streambeds. Semi-precious, gemstone varieties.

Clear quartz (rock crystal)

Colourless, glassy. Transparent.

Amethyst

Transparent to semi-transparent. Purple to delicate pink, sometimes with white banding and colour zoning.

Smoky quartz (cairngorm)

Transparent to semi-transparent. Smoky yellow, brown to black.

Citrine

Transparent. Pale yellow to amber. Sometimes called false topaz.

QUARTZ *(Cryptocrystalline varieties)*

Hardness: 6 to 7. Possible fluctuation in hardness due to impurities.

Flint

Opaque to translucent. Grey, brown to black. Found as irregular nodules in chalk, also as pebbles on beaches and in streambeds.

Chert

Opaque to translucent. White, smoky yellow to brown. Close similarity to flint but occurs in layers.

Sard

Opaque, reddish brown chalcedony.

Jasper

Opaque. Variations of red to brown, yellow to green. Form of chalcedony fused with coloured clays. Colour depends on mineral content of impurities. Sometimes contains ribbons of clear chalcedony through the stone with appearance of suspended particles. Takes a good polish but liable to undercutting in softer parts.

Chalcedony

Translucent, occasionally opalescent. Milky white to pale blue. Waxy lustre. Found in nodules and veins.

Carnelian

Translucent. Pale to deep red chalcedony. Waxy appearance. Nodules show pitted and gnarled surface—an aid to identification in all chalcedony varieties.

Agate varieties (Figure 4)

Characterised by strong banding. Can be semi-transparent to opaque. Wide colour range, white, pink, red, yellow, blue and dark brown. Also, clear chalcedony, carnelian and jasper agates.

Banded agate

Section through a nodule will show even variegated banding, usually conforming to perimeter shape.

Fortification agate

Banding with angular changes of pattern, resembling ground-plan of a fortress.

Orbicular or eyed agate

Banding in small circular patterns or concentric rings.

Onyx

Straight, alternating bands of white and coloured chalcedony.

Sardonyx
Layered combination of white chalcedony and sard. Rare.
Moss agate
Chalcedony showing fern or moss-like impurities within the stone.

Other quartz pebbles, common on beaches, in streambeds and gravel deposits

Quartzite (metamorphic sandstone)
Opaque. White, yellow to brown. Tints of purple and blue due to mineral staining. Re-crystalised quartz grains of coarse sandstones, strongly fused into a tough finely textured stone.

4 Agate varieties. Sections through agate nodules
a Banded agate, showing small crystal geode in the centre **b** Banded agate, with straight onyx formation in lower half **c** Fortification agate **d** Eyed or orbicular agate **e** Further example of eyed agate **f** Moss agate

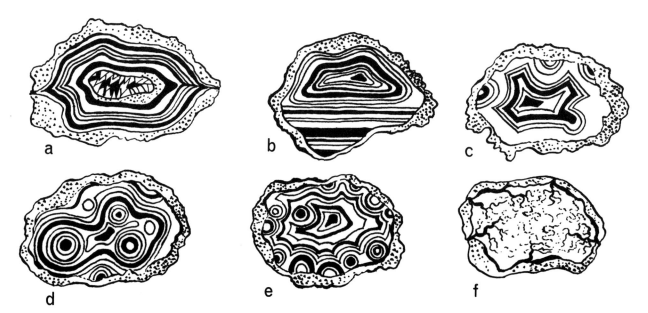

Milky quartz

Opaque to translucent. White to creamy yellow. Crystalline material often found as veins on other stones, also very common as beach pebbles. Polishes well but fractures if overheated.

Crystalline banded quartz

Pebbles are opaque to translucent in section. White to yellowish brown. Multi-coloured impurities provide intricate patterns and banding. Crystalline structure strongly evident when cut and polished.

Stones recognisable by their distinctive pattern or texture (Figure 5)

Conglomerate (puddingstone)

Opaque. Multi-coloured, rounded pebbles of various rock fragments cemented together in fine-textured matrix.

Quartz breccia

Opaque. Angular fragments of rock bound together in a siliceous matrix which often displays attractive network patterns. Occasionally contains minute crystal geodes.

Porphyry

Characterised by pattern of large crystals embedded in a compact groundmass of fine-grained material.

Granite

Various tints of red and grey. Coarse to finely textured aggregate of the minerals, feldspar, quartz and mica. Pebbles widespread.

Laurvikite

Hardness: 6. Grey to black with flashes of blue (schiller) when viewed from different angles. Of Scandinavian origin, transported to England in glacial deposits. Pebbles frequent in the boulder clays of the East Coast. The attractive blue schiller makes this a popular facing stone for buildings when polished.

Other minerals of special interest

Serpentine

Hardness: $2\frac{1}{2}$ to 4. Opaque. Colour varies from pale to dark green, red to brown. Mottled, and veined with white. Smooth, waxy or soapy to touch. Soft, with tendency to undercut or flake. Semi-precious serpentine used for jewellery and ornamental purposes.

Fluorspar (fluorite)

Hardness: 4. Transparent to translucent. Colourless, purple, green to blue. Cubic crystal groups or in massive formation. Some varieties are fluorescent in ultraviolet light. Soft and easily fractured.

Fluorspar (variety Blue John)

Hardness: 4. Semi-transparent to opaque. Blue, purple and yellow with attractive banding. Semi-precious, becoming rare. Used for jewellery and ornamental purposes since Roman times. Very brittle, requires immersion in resin to bind the crystalline structure prior to shaping and polishing.

Garnet

Hardness: 6 to 7. Many types of garnet, from precious to common. Transparent to opaque. Red or brownish red, green. Found as crystals. Associated with wide range of igneous and metamorphic rocks. Crushed garnet used for abrasive purposes.

Haematite (kidney ore)

Hardness: $5\frac{1}{2}$ to $6\frac{1}{2}$. Opaque. Black to red. Fibrous structure, silky lustre. Found as kidney formation. Gives red streak on white unglazed tile. Soft to grind and polish but very messy due to red iron content.

Iron pyrites (fool's gold)

Hardness: 6 to $6\frac{1}{2}$. Opaque. Found as brassy yellow crystals, as fossil replacement or as speckled inclusions in other rocks and minerals. Not usually cut and polished but natural crystals attractive set in jewellery.

Marcasite

Hardness: 6 to $6\frac{1}{2}$. Opaque. Metallic. Less yellow than pyrites, with radiating crystal structure. Found in nodules and tabular formations in clays and chalk.

Marble

Usually calcite. Hardness: 3. Various colours. Soft and compact. Polishes well. Used mainly for ornamental purposes. Iona, Portsoy and Connemara Marbles are really forms of semi-precious serpentine. In addition to architectural uses, they are polished for jewellery by local craftsmen.

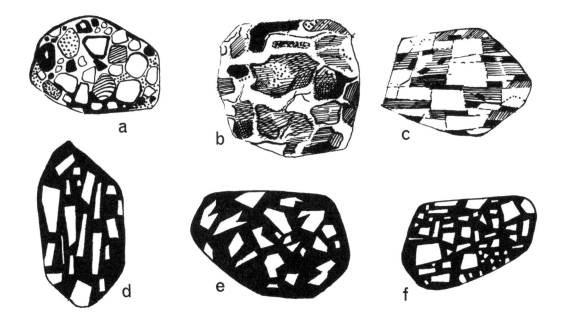

5 Pebbles recognised by distinctive pattern or texture
a Puddingstone **b** Breccia. Varieties of conglomerate **c** Laurvikite
d, e, f Types of rhomb-porphyry

Semi-precious material of organic origin

Jet (fossilised wood)

Hardness 3½. Opaque. Intense black. Very light in weight. Gives brown streak on white unglazed tile. Burns with blue flame. Has oily content. Can be found as water-worn pebbles or in thin seams on North Yorkshire coast. Extremely tough but soft enough to carve. Polishes to a high gloss.

Amber (fossilised resin)

Hardness: 2½ to 3. Transparent to opaque. Very light in weight. Pale yellow to dark red. Occasionally contains petrified insects and plant fragments. Burns with smoky flame, aromatic. Feels warm to touch and floats in strong saline solution. Of Baltic origin, carried by tides and currents to East Anglian coast.

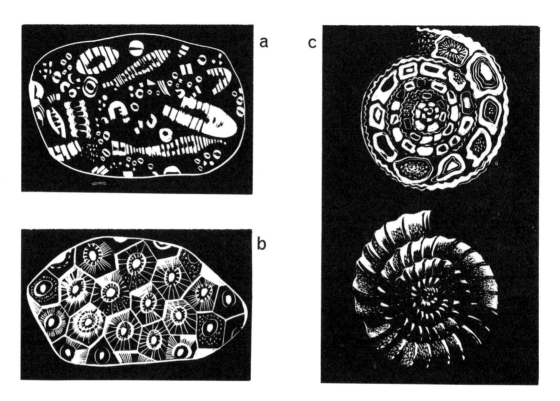

6 Pattern analysis of polished fossil material
a Crinoidal limestone. Fragments of crinoids (sea lilies) **b** Fossil coral with distinct hexagonal structure **c** Ammonite. *Top* Polished section showing spiral formation with internal mineral replacement *Bottom* External appearance

Other fossilised material

Hardness depends on the mineral which has replaced the fossil and the matrix. The various forms of fossilised material to be found in the original bedding or as smooth beach pebbles shows evidence of life which existed millions of years ago. The intricacies of shape and pattern revealed in polished specimens are shown in the pattern analysis (figure 6) also photograph. Figure 7. Many, so-called, marbles and decorative building stones show a high concentration of fossilised coral and shell fragments.

Locations for collecting

Beaches are the most accessible and rewarding areas for collecting stones, but allowances must be made for variations in climate and local geology. Many beaches are conditioned by tides at certain times of the year and it is possible to find drifts of sand and silt covering good shingle beds periodically. Erosion and excessive storm damage contribute to change of coastline in areas bounded by cliffs or hills composed of boulder clay, and there is a constant renewal of material for the collector.

Shingle deposits in streams, rivers and estuaries are worth investigating and a study of regional geology may provide clues to collecting possibilities. Mine spoil heaps, quarries, cuttings and other artificial exposures are excellent sources for collecting geological specimens but in terms of polishing material random exploration of these areas may prove frustrating. Mines and quarries producing specific types of minerals and ornamental stones should only be visited by special arrangement with the owners.

Pebbles of jasper and the more common quartz varieties are so widely distributed around the coast that, in order to avoid tedious repetition, reference to collecting areas for these has been limited.

The following selection of stones and locations will provide a lead for the collector and encourage further exploration.

ENGLAND

Amethyst
  Cornwall Beach near Marazion, Carn Brea Mine near Cambourne
  Northumberland The Cheviot and nearby hills
  Yorkshire Pebbles of amethystine quartz occasionally found on East coast beaches
Cairngorm and Citrine
  Cornwall Beach near Marazion
  Devon Hills east of Moretonhampstead
  Yorkshire As pebbles on East coast beaches

Agates and Carnelians
  Cornwall On beaches at Porthleven and Marazion, Kynance Cove, Godrevy Point and St Ives Bay
  Devon Budleigh Salterton, Sidmouth
  Dorset Chesil Bank near Abbotsbury
  Hampshire Isle of Wight, beaches between Sandown and Ventnor
  Kent Beaches between Sandwich and Deal
  Lancashire Walney Island
  Norfolk Cromer and Sheringham beaches
  Somerset Between Clevedon and Portishead
  Suffolk Aldeburgh, Landguard Point south of Felixstowe
  Sussex Pevensey Bay, Eastbourne
  Yorkshire Most bays between Whitby and Spurn Point will yield small agate and carnelian pebbles, in particular, Stoupe Beck, Carnelian Bay, Filey, Reighton Gap, Atwick, Hornsea
Serpentine
  Cornwall Lizard peninsula
Fluorspar
  Cumberland Near Alston
  Co. Durham Weardale
  Cornwall Old mine workings near St Ives, St Just, Callington and Marazion
  Derbyshire Blue John variety found at Castleton
  Yorkshire Old mine workings near Grassington and Pateley Bridge
Jet
  Yorkshire Found in seams in Whitby district. Also as water-worn pebbles on East coast beaches
Amber
  Yorkshire East coast beaches
  Norfolk Beaches
  Suffolk Beaches

WALES

Agates and Carnelians
  Anglesey Cymmeron Bay
  Caernarvon Southern beaches of Lleyn Peninsula

Cardigan   Beaches between New Quay and Aberystwyth
Pembrokeshire   Beaches on North Pembrokeshire coast
Serpentine
Anglesey   Holy Island, Cymmeron Bay

SCOTLAND

Amethyst
  Angus   Scurdie Ness near Montrose. Usan, in agate nodules
  Argyll   Hills north of Campbeltown
  Ayrshire   Kaim Hill, near Largs
  Kirkudbrightshire   Waterworn pebbles in streams near Dalbeattie. Kippford. Near Needles Eye, Glenburn near New Abbey, Kinharvie
  Ross and Cromarty   Contin, Garve
  Sutherland   Quinag near Kylisku, Glen Dunrobin, Golspie
Cairngorm (smoky quartz)
  Aberdeenshire   In red granite quarries and granite veins, south of Peterhead. Culblean, Deeside
  Angus   Usan near Montrose
  Argyll   Hills north of Campbeltown
  Banffshire   Cairngorm and nearby mountains, in mountain streams and in the bed of the River Avon
  Fifeshire   Hills near Luthrie
  Kirkudbrightshire   Hills near Dalbeattie
  Ross and Cromarty   Contin, Garve
  Sutherland   Glen Dunrobin, Golspie, Quinag near Kylisku
Agates and Carnelians
  Angus   Montrose, Ferryden, Scurdie Ness, Usan
  Ayrshire   South of Heads of Ayr, Dunure, River Irvine nr Darvel
  East Lothian   River Tyne near Haddington, beach at Dunbar
  Fifeshire   Shores of the River Tay, Balmerino. Wormit
  Kincardineshire   St Cyrus, Kinneff
  Midlothian   Pentland Hills near Carlops
  Perthshire   Ochil Hills, Path of Condie
  Sutherland $1\frac{1}{2}$ miles south of Cape Wrath, Ardmair Bay near Ullapool

Agate
Amethyst

CARLISLE
ALSTON
Fluorspar

Garnet   Fluorspar

WHITBY
Jet   Jet
Agate
SCARBOROUGH   Carnelian
Citrine

Jasper   BARROW
Agate

Fluorspar   YORK

Agate
Carnelian
Jasper
Agate
Citrine
SPURN HD.

PRESTON

LEEDS   HULL

ANGLESEY

LIVERPOOL

SHEFFIELD

Serpentine   Jasper
Agate
CAERNARVON

CASTLETON
Fluorspar
Blue John

Jasper
PORTMADOC

Agate

DERBY

Agate
Amber
Jasper
Carnelian
Amber
Citrine
Jasper
Carnelian
Agate

NORWICH

Jasper
Agate
CARDIGAN

BIRMINGHAM

LONDON

CARDIFF   BRISTOL
Jasper

Jasper   Agate

Agate
Carnelian
Jasper

BUDE   LYME
REGIS   BOURNEMOUTH   BRIGHTON

Cairngorm   Agate
Agate Jasper

Agate
Jasper

Agate   Fluorspar   Agate
Amethyst
Amethyst
Cairngorm
Agate
Jasper   TORQUAY

LIZARD
Serpentine

Agate
Jasper

28

Garnets (widely distributed)

    Fifeshire Elie Ness

    Ross and Cromarty Contin, Garve

    Sutherland Kildonan, Struie, Bettyhill, Ben Hope

Serpentine

    Ayrshire Ballantrae, Lendalfoot

    Banffshire Portsoy

    Hebrides Iona, Tiree

    Perthshire Glen Tilt

    Sutherland Inchnadamph, Kylisku, Scourie

Safety precautions

The importance of safety precautions during field trips cannot be over-emphasised and the following suggestions will be helpful to collectors in coastal and inland areas.

Information about tidal conditions must be obtained before making any beach excursion, and sufficient time allowed to complete the project in hand. Beaches backed by high cliffs offer little means of escape, and features known to geologists as wave-cut platforms demand extra care when the tide is backed by an onshore wind.

Hammering at, or climbing, a cliff face which is susceptible to erosion can lead to disaster, and however attractive an embedded specimen may be, priority must be given to personal safety and consideration for others in the immediate vicinity.

When collecting in quarries, avoid the working faces and overhanging blocks of stone or boulders. These may be unstable due to blasting operations or because of erosion in the case of disused sites. Abandoned mine shafts are particularly dangerous and collecting should be done on the old spoil heaps where specimens of sufficient interest can usually be found.

Where possible, ensure that others have knowledge of proposed routes to be taken in mountainous or moorland areas, and the use of map and compass is an added precaution in changeable weather conditions.

Some inland collecting areas may be on private property and permission to visit these must be obtained. Technically, all specimens found are the property of the landowners, but only in rare circumstances do they insist on their rights of possession.

Equipment

Adequate clothing and footwear should be selected to suit conditions. Nailed boots or strong shoes are recommended for hills or rocky terrain and wellington or rubber boots for beaches and streams.

On a brief visit to the beach, all that may be needed is a polythene bag to hold a few choice specimens, but for planned excursions of longer duration the following items of equipment can be regarded as basic:

Small haversack or duffle-bag

Polythene bags, tissues or newspaper for wrapping specimens

Geologists' hammer

Small chisel

Penknife

Small magnifying lens

Notebook and pencil, for recording locations

Compass and maps

Small first-aid kit

For visits to quarries, a protective helmet is a useful item of equipment, and goggles are an additional safeguard when hammering rocks.

7 Examples of polished fossil material

Serpentine

Amber

Fluorspar

Jet

Jasper

granite

Chalcedony

garnet

Conglomerate

Polishing Stones by Hand

A clear distinction must be made between polishing stones by hand and the skilled craft of lapidary involving machines. Polishing by hand requires minimum equipment and for many collectors this simpler method will solve the problems of cost and space. The basic requirements are an abrasive, obtained in graded powder form, and a polishing agent such as tin oxide or cerium oxide.

Polishing flat sections and stones with evenly curved surfaces presents few problems, and a careful selection of smooth water-worn pebbles is recommended. These should be large enough to hold comfortably, keeping the fingertips out of contact with the abrasive materials. Thin slabs of stone, which have been trimmed on a diamond saw, can be gummed to a wooden block for easy handling.

Polishing a flat surface

Materials

  Silicon carbide abrasive grits, grades 220, 320, 500.
  Polishing agent. Tin oxide or cerium oxide.
  Small sheet of plate glass, for phases one and two.
  Sheet of perspex or leather, for phase three.
  Thick felt pad, for polishing phase.

Sanding : phase one. 220 grade abrasive grit
Apply half a teaspoonful of grit over the surface of the plate glass and moisten with a little water. Press the stone firmly to the glass and rotate steadily, distributing the grit over the entire surface of the plate. Renewal of grit will be necessary during the process owing

Facing   Unpolished and polished examples of stones from British locations
1st row   Three varieties of serpentine
2nd row   Amber   Fluorspar   Fluorspar (Blue John)
3rd row   Jet   Jasper pebble   Shap granite with iron pyrities
4th row   Chalcedony in limestone   Common garnet   Conglomerate

33

to the breakdown of particles in grinding. Periodically wash the stone in clean water and check on the progress. Using circular movements, clockwise and anti-clockwise, continue grinding until the face of the stone is level and free from pitted or concave areas.

Sanding : phase two. 320 *grade abrasive grit*
Wash the stone, plate glass and hands thoroughly, removing all traces of the previous grit.

Apply 320 grit to the plate, keeping the surface damp. Too much water will float the grit particles and lessen the abrasive action. Repeat the sanding operation as in phase one, using moderate pressure, continuing until the stone is smooth. Avoid rushing the early stages, as the length of time spent on phases one and two will influence the final result.

Sanding : phase three. 500 grade abrasive grit
Wash thoroughly as before. Store the glass plate safely away and clean up the working area to avoid contact with coarser grits.

A softer or slightly more resilient surface is required at this stage to hold the abrasive particles and prevent the stone merely sliding over the polishing plate. Obtain a sheet of thick perspex and score the surface with coarse sandpaper. Alternatively, glue a square of shoe-leather, rough side uppermost, to a firm support such as hardboard or plywood. The grit will become effectively embedded in these two surfaces and need not be washed away each time after use. A polythene bag can be used for storage to avoid contamination with other grits.

Sprinkle 500 grit on to the prepared surface and dampen with a few drops of water. Keeping the stone perfectly flat, continue the action as before and inspect the progress frequently. Depending on the degree of thoroughness during each stage, the stone should now have a smooth flat surface and begin to show a dull lustre.

As an alternative method, it is possible to carry out the three sanding phases using graded silicon carbide papers instead of loose grits.

Polishing phase
Before commencing on this final stage, remove all previous materials and wash away all traces of grit from the working area.

A good finish is obtained using a pad of thick hard felt but soft leather or suede, mounted on a firm support, will also produce successful results. For the polishing agent, mix a thin paste of tin oxide or cerium oxide with water in a shallow dish. Dampen the pad slightly and apply the polishing mixture with a soft brush. Never mix different types of polish on the same pad.

Rub the stone vigorously on the pad until the frictional heat dries up the moisture, causing dragging. At this stage, speed up the polishing action, decreasing pressure on the stone and skimming the surface of the pad. Continue until a satisfactory polish has been achieved. Apply polishing paste as required but do not saturate the pad as polishing or glazing occurs when the surface is almost dry.

Polishing a curved surface

Materials
>   Silicon carbide grit powders, grades 220, 320, 500 or 600.
>   Polishing agent. Tin oxide or cerium oxide.
>   Small ovenglass dish and thick 'opal glass' jars.
>   Strips of thin leather.
>   Thick felt pad.

Sanding : phase one. 220 grade abrasive grit
Obtain a shallow ovenglass dish with curved interior, large enough to allow free movement of hand and stone. Small 'opal glass' jars of the type used for meat pastes are ideal for small pebbles which are mounted on dopsticks, (see chapter on dopping stones).

Moisten the dish or jar with water and apply 220 grit. Select a suitable pebble, preferably one which is free from cracks or holes. Using round, stroking movements, with moderate pressure, rotate the stone on the curved grinding surface of the dish. When sanding a small pebble on a dopstick, use a stirring motion while holding the stick with the fingertips close to the stone. Wash and inspect the stone frequently and continue sanding until it is quite smooth.

Sanding : phase two. 320 grade abrasive grit
Wash the dish or jar thoroughly and clean away all traces of the previous grit. Introduce 320 grit into the same dish as before and repeat the sanding operation.

Sanding : phase three. 500 or 600 grade abrasive grit
The leather pad suggested for use in phase three for flat surfaces can

also be used for a curved stone by using stroking and rocking movements. A curved pad can be made by glueing a piece of thin pliable leather, rough side uppermost, round the inside of the dish. An easy 'peel-off' type of gum can be used if only one dish is available.

Apply the 500 or 600 grit and moisten with water but do not over soak the pad. Using a circular stroking action, apply fluctuating pressures. Rotate and rock the stone at the same time, distributing the treatment over the whole surface. At this stage some stones will acquire a semi-polish but sanding must be continued until all marks and scratches have been erased.

Final polishing
Wash the stone carefully and clean away all traces of sanding materials. Using tin oxide or cerium oxide, applied in a thin paste to the thick felt or soft leather pads kept solely for this purpose, continue working with a circular stroking action until the stone is polished to satisfaction.

Building machines for cutting and polishing

Cutting a stone refers to the act of grinding rough material to a desired shape by means of power-driven wheels or discs. This is followed by progressive stages of sanding prior to the final polishing operation. Wheels and discs are mounted on a shaft geared to revolve at different speeds and powered by a small motor. Machines for every lapidary process are now manufactured but, using basic manufactured components, suitable machines can be built at home or in a school workshop at little cost. (Figure 8.)

In planning a machine, electrical considerations are important. During grinding, the wheel is in contact with water and a certain amount of spray or splashing is inevitable, for this reason the motor should be positioned behind the machine or given adequate protection. In the home-made portable models (Figures 9 and 11) the motors are completely boxed in as an extra safety precaution. In addition, it is advisable to have a push button On/Off switch attached to the machine for convenience and emergency.

Basic components

Electric motor $\frac{1}{4}$ hp (186·5 watts)   Re-conditioned washing-machine motors can usually be obtained cheaply.

Shaft with $\frac{1}{2}$ in or $\frac{3}{4}$ in (12 or 18 mm) arbor   Can be bought with or without ballrace bearings.

Pulleys   Triple pulleys for varying speed ratios. Fitted on to motor spindle and shaft.

V belt drive from motor to shaft   Length of belt depending on construction and position of motor.

Silicon carbide grinding wheels 60, 120 and 220 grades   Recommended size, 6 in x 1 in (152 x 25 mm). Correct arbor size should be quoted when ordering wheels.

Push button On/Off switches

Accessories

Water coolant Metal canister, plastic bottle or similar container to form overhead drip-feed to grinding wheel.

Plastic box To contain surplus water from the wheel.

Splash guard Can be made of perspex by heating and bending into shape.

Wire mesh guard Exposed pulleys, belts, projecting shafts or spindles must be covered by a guard.

Plastic bowl Used in construction of horizontal machine.

Plastic squeezy bottles For application of abrasive grits and water.

Materials used in construction

The frame can be of wood fixed to a substantial base. Alternatively, light metal or perforated angle iron can be bought already sawn into lengths, together with an assortment of nuts and bolts. Plywood or similar material can be used for the frame covering, finished with a polyurethane lacquer or paint for easy cleaning. Remember to allow access to screws and bolts for maintenance purposes. Nuts and bolts should be used in the construction wherever possible, and particular attention should be paid to securing the shaft bearings, which are subject to vibration during grinding and tension from the driving belt.

Figures 9 and 11 illustrate efficient home-made machines for grinding and polishing, but variations in design and construction can be adapted to facilities and materials available. For this reason, and to avoid limitation, specific dimensions have been omitted. Using the size of motor, shaft and bearings as a starting point, the machine can be worked out proportionately.

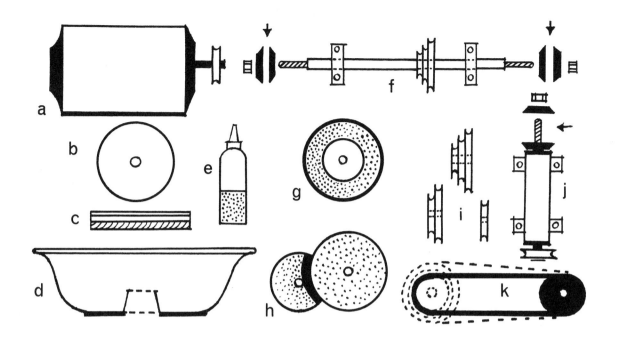

8 Diagram illustrating some of the equipment discussed in this chapter
a ¼ hp motor **b** Thick felt polishing disc 6 in (152 mm) diameter **c** Home-made circular sanding discs 6 in diameter, consisting of plywood base, felt and leather **d** Plastic bowl, with beaker cut in half and wedged in the base **e** Small plastic bottle to contain clear water or abrasive mixture **f** and **j** Alternative types of shaft obtainable for turning discs and grinding wheels. Wheels and discs are supported between metal collars indicated by arrows, and secured to the arbor by a nut **g** Silicon carbide grinding wheel, 6 in (152 mm) diameter by 1 in (25 mm) thick **h** Wet/dry, abrasive paper or cloth discs **i** Pulleys, can be bought singly or in fixed multiples **k** Vee belt, to run from motor to shaft

Construction of vertical sanding discs

Sanding discs can be made for use on the vertical machine, following the grinding and shaping stages. For the base, use a disc of thick perspex, plywood or metal, drilled with a centre hole corresponding to the arbor size. Thick rubber, glued to the base, will form a resilient pad upon which graded silicon carbide discs of paper or cloth are gummed as required.

9 Vertical grinding and polishing machine. Portable table model. External appearance
a Alternative methods for applying water coolant **b** Perspex splash guard **c** Silicon carbide grinding wheel **d** Small wad of newspaper clipped to splash guard to prevent spray **e** Plastic tray to hold surplus water from wheel and sponge for cleaning stone **f** Push button on/off switches **g** Direction of grinding wheel when revolving

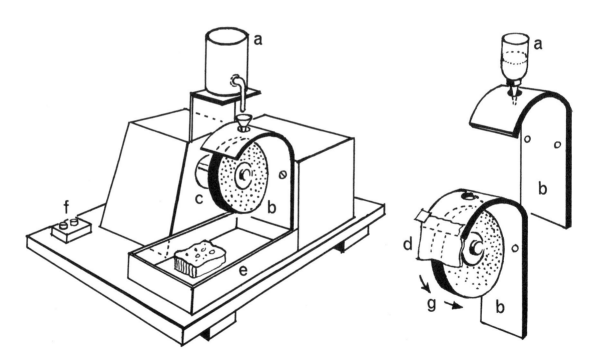

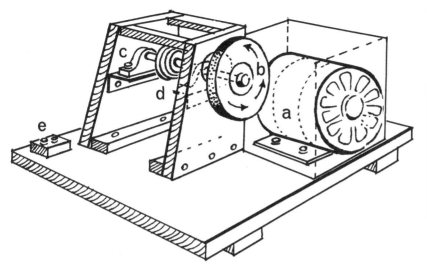

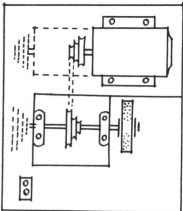

10 Vertical grinding and polishing machine. Showing internal construction
a ¼ hp motor **b** Grinding wheel, showing direction of movement **c** Shaft
bearings mounted on angle iron **d** Triple pulleys, 2 in, 3 in, 4 in (50, 76, 101
mm) on shaft **e** Push button on/off switch
Construction mainly of wood on a stout base. Rubber feet fitted underneath.
Holes can be drilled in one of the panels boxing in the motor to allow circula-
tion of air.
Plan Showing positions of motor, pulleys and shaft. Dotted lines show
alternative position of motor and pulleys moved across to the left. This would
require a wire mesh safety guard over the pulleys and belt

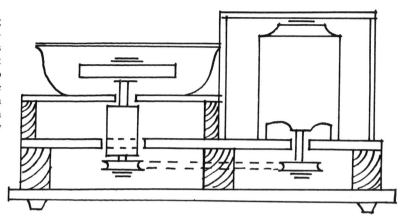

11 Horizontal sanding and polishing machine. Portable table model. Construction of wood. Motor and working parts covered for safety. Diagram shows a short sealed shaft with ball race, requiring no maintenance. Type of motor required here must have end mounting. Sanding disc in position, turning inside plastic bowl with hole cut for shaft. Rubber feet fixed below to deaden sound and prevent movement

Construction of lapping discs

Sanding with loose abrasive grits is done on horizontal laps and a separate lap must be made for each grit size used. To prepare the lapping disc, obtain a piece of shoe-leather and cut a 6 in (152 mm) diameter circle. Glue this, rough side uppermost, on to a firm support such as perspex or plywood cut to the same size and drilled with a centre hole to fit the arbor.

For the finer grits a more resilient surface is preferable and a disc of carpet underfelt or thick rubber is sandwiched between base and leather. In this case, the leather should be thinner and more pliable, also glued with the rough side uppermost.

Polishing buffs

As a general purpose polishing buff, thick hard felt is the most satisfactory material. Circular discs of felt, half-inch thickness, can be obtained from lapidary suppliers, and glued to a support. The felt buffs can be fitted to either the vertical or horizontal machines. An additional buff of soft leather should be made, to be used for soft or heat-sensitive stones.

Construction details

Superstructure housing grinding unit, bolted to desk lid, allowing whole unit to hinge back for inspection

Desk lid with hole for driving belt

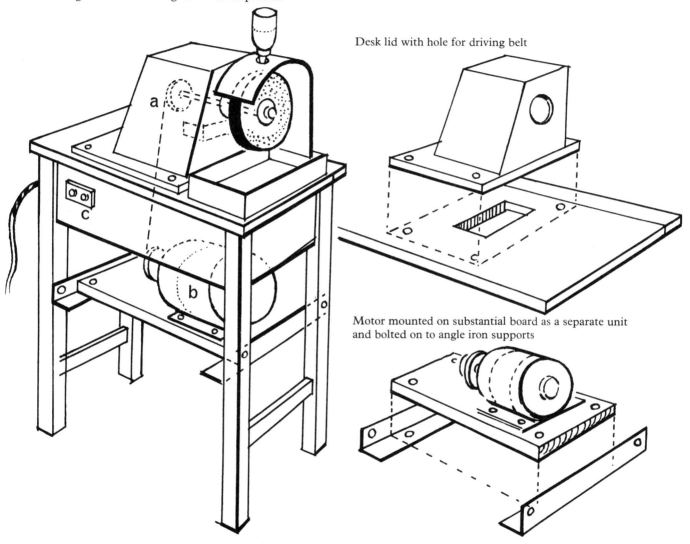

Motor mounted on substantial board as a separate unit and bolted on to angle iron supports

12 Grinding and polishing machine. Desk conversion
a The grinding unit **b** Electric motor mounted below **c** On/off switch

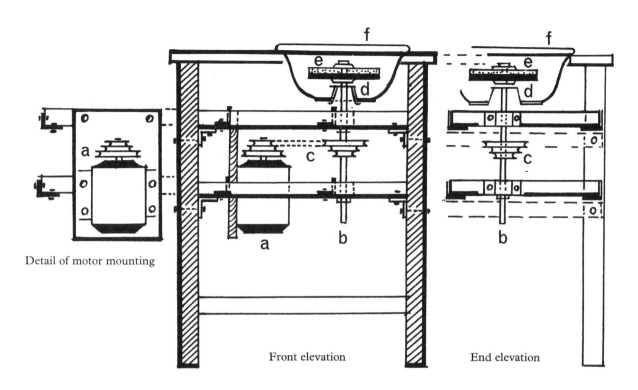

Detail of motor mounting

Front elevation   End elevation

13 Horizontal sanding and polishing machine. Desk conversion. Angle iron framework bolted to existing desk structure **a** ¼ hp motor mounted in vertical position **b** Shaft **c** Triple pulleys, 2 in, 3 in, 4 in (50, 76, 101 mm) on motor and shaft **d** Plastic beaker cut in half and inserted in base of bowl. This prevents any water or grit reaching the shaft bearings **e** Leather sanding disc in position, held by metal collars and nut **f** Plastic bowl wedged into hole cut in desk lid. To wash bowl between grit changes, remove disc and lift bowl clear of shaft. Desk lid can be hinged back for inspection and maintenance of working parts

44

Machines built into desks

Modernisation in schools often results in replacement of desks, and for teachers and pupils intending to make lapidary machines an old desk can provide a substantial ready-made framework. The superstructure shown in figure 12, is bolted as a unit to the desk lid. By releasing the pulley belt, the lid and grinding unit can be hinged back for inspection of the motor. In the horizontal sanding and polishing machine, (figure 13) the conversion is even simpler. A hole is cut in the lid of the desk to accommodate a plastic bowl, and framework is added below to secure the motor and shaft.

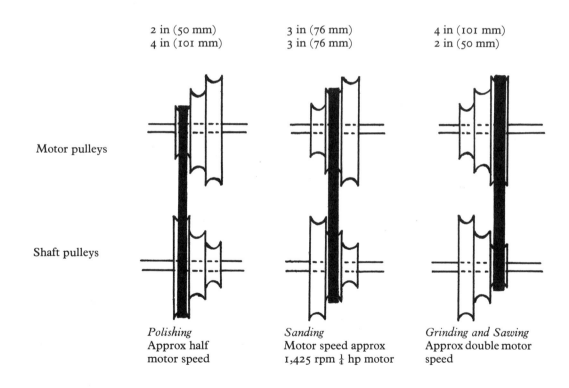

2 in (50 mm)
4 in (101 mm)

3 in (76 mm)
3 in (76 mm)

4 in (101 mm)
2 in (50 mm)

Motor pulleys

Shaft pulleys

Polishing
Approx half
motor speed

Sanding
Motor speed approx
1,425 rpm ¼ hp motor

Grinding and Sawing
Approx double motor
speed

14 Belt positions for speed changes

Manufactured lapidary machines

These are two examples of the many types of lapidary machines designed and manufactured, and which are used by schools, evening classes and lapidary clubs.

Grinding and polishing machine (figure 15)   The position of the wheels enables two people to grind stones simultaneously. The sanding discs, shown at rear, are fitted on to the extended shaft. Photograph shows polishing disc in position, with guard. When in use, grinding wheels run in troughs of water.

Flat lap (figure 16)   This cast iron lap is used for sanding and polishing flat surfaces. It is of compact design with the motor incorporated beneath the fibreglass tray.

Tumbling machines and diamond saws are also being manufactured and can be obtained through lapidary suppliers.

15   Grinding and polishing machine

16   Flat lap

Building a diamond saw

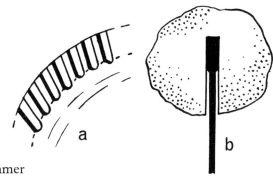

a Detail of notched rim diamond saw blade
b Saw blade clearance as cutting proceeds. Allow for this clearance when marking out or cutting a special size of stone

One way of obtaining small pieces for shaping is by using a hammer to break large stones, but with this method fracturing and wastage is inevitable, especially with the more brittle varieties. For this reason, most amateur lapidaries eventually obtain a diamond saw to prepare pieces of stone of workable size. While there are several types of manufactured machines available for sawing rocks, effective substitutes can be constructed using basic components, of which the most expensive item is the diamond saw blade.

The type of blade widely used is the notched-rim variety, consisting of a thin metal disc notched or burred on the rim. Diamond grits are embedded in the notches, which are then closed to seal in the grit particles. Some blades contain a mixture of diamond grit and powdered metal fused into the notches by a heating process. The notches on each side provide a good clearance for the blade during cutting. (Figure 17.) Unlike other saw blades, the diamond saw has no teeth and cutting is done by the diamond particles biting into the stone. With careful use the blades give good service, only ceasing to be effective when the diamond is worn away.

Basic requirements

Diamond saw blade. 6 in or 8 in (152 or 203 mm) for trimming. 10 in (254 mm) upwards for slabbing.
Steel discs or washers to support the blade.
Shaft and pulley. $\frac{1}{2}$ in or $\frac{5}{8}$ in for 6 in or 8 in (12 or 16 mm for 152 or 203 mm) blades. Thicker shafts for larger blades.
$\frac{1}{4}$ hp (186·5 watts) motor and V belt drive.
Steel saw bed, with narrow slot for blade, and drainage holes.
Leak-proof tank to contain coolant mixture. Must be substantial.
Splash guards over saw blade and at the front.
Light oil as coolant and lubricant. Low viscosity essential.

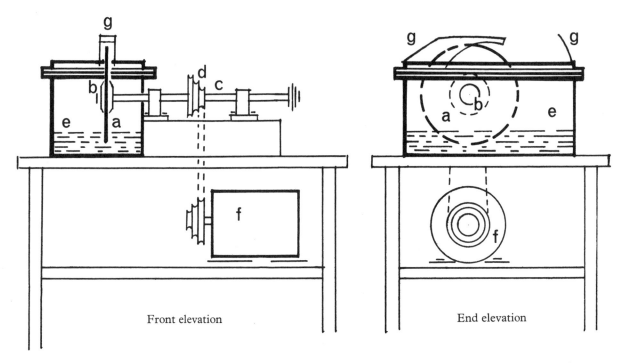

Front elevation   End elevation

18 Assembly of diamond saw. Fixed bench construction with motor mounted below
a Saw blade **b** Metal discs to support blade **c** Shaft, single or double ended
d Pulley **e** Tank with coolant **f** $\frac{1}{4}$ hp motor **g** Splash guards

Facing Polished and unpolished examples of British beach pebbles
Top Citrines Carnelians Quartz pebbles
Centre Scottish agates Clear chalcedony Tumble-polished quartz pebbles
Bottom Tumble-polished jasper pebbles Shaped stones of jasper and serpentine Polished specimens of conglomerates

Citrine

Carnelian

quartz

Agates

clear chalcedony

quartz

Jasper

Serpentine

Parts are assembled as illustrated in figures 18 and 19. This differs little from other types of circular saws and can be constructed to individual requirements.

The saw blade revolves between 1425 and 3000 r.p.m. and runs through an oily fluid in a leak-proof tank, the rim of the blade being immersed to a depth of ½ in (12 mm). The type of coolant recommended by manufacturers of diamond blades is usually obtainable from lapidary suppliers. Soluble oils and water, as used on metalwork lathes, can be used but the saw must be cleaned and wiped with an oily rag after use or rusting will occur.

A considerable force of spray occurs within the tank as the blade revolves in the fluid and necessitates a leak-proof joint between the tank and sawbed. The size of any drainage holes in the tank cover, and the saw aperture must be kept to a minimum. The splash guard over the blade must be as close as possible to counteract spraying and direct excess fluid on to the blade. (Figure 20.) A spray guard must also be fitted to the front of the sawbed. Raised flanges round the edge of the sawbed will contain the pool of oil which forms during sawing.

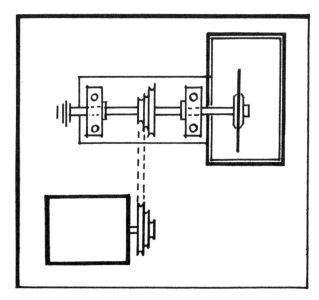

Plan

19 Alternative arrangement for diamond saw. Portable model with motor mounted in rear. A wire mesh guard for belt and pulley is essential in this design

20 Detail of diamond saw, showing splash guard construction. This can be of thick perspex or metal, and made to raise or lower as required

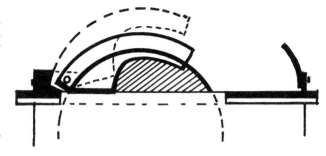

Side elevation

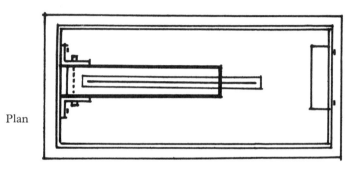

Plan

How to use the saw

Sawing uneven pieces of rock into slices is known as slabbing and for this the larger size of saw blade should be used, but pebbles and small rocks up to 2 in (50 mm) in diameter can be slabbed with a 6 in (152 mm) blade. The stone can be held in the fingers during cutting with complete safety but the use of a home-made rock clamp (figure 21) can make the task easier and ensure a cleaner cut. Some manufactured machines have a built-in feed clamp running along a guide rail.

Holding the stone firmly between forefinger and thumb of both hands, slide it gently on the sawbed towards the revolving blade. Only a light pressure should be used at first, increasing as cutting proceeds. The amount of pressure required depends on the material being cut, and too much as well as too little pressure will cancel out the cutting action. Experience will enable the operator to feel when the bite of the diamond grit is cutting correctly. If flashes of light or sparks are observed at the point of contact between saw and stone, it can mean either, too much pressure is being used, causing excessive friction, or the height of the coolant in the tank is insufficient and may require topping up. In both conditions, cutting will have ceased and there is a possibility of grinding away the tip of the metal disc, thus shortening the life of the blade.

Do not attempt to change direction of cut halfway through the operation as this can cause severe damage to the blade. There is also a tendency for the stone to ride up the saw, resulting in wobbling which can cause a permanent twist to the blade. This can be avoided by holding the stone firmly on the sawbed. When the saw is nearing the end of the cut, ease off the pressure a little, and at the point of break-through pull the stone back sharply from the blade.

A bowl of warm water and detergent should be kept on hand to

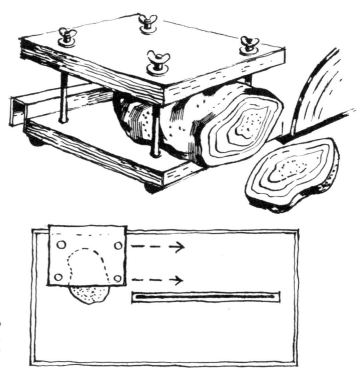

21 Home-made rock clamp, designed to run along raised flange of the sawbed. Half-round metal runners fixed underneath for easy movement

wash the film of oil off the stones after cutting. Some of the more porous types of stone absorb oil quickly and should be washed immediately.

Trimming into shape

Having slabbed a rock into slices, the next step is to cut the thin slabs into workable shapes and for this a smaller diameter blade can be used. All the points mentioned for slabbing apply to trimming, and the slices are fed to the saw by hand. (Figure 22.) The flat face of the stone should run smoothly on the sawbed, which must be free from sludge or fragments of rock.

Care of the saw

Repeated sawing of agate or material of similar hardness can have a glazing effect on the diamond particles, which results in sliding or skidding. When this happens the blade can be re-sharpened by cutting through pieces of soft sand brick, which cleans up the diamond points. Reversing the blade occasionally is also recommended for conditioning the saw.

It is important to clean out the tank periodically and dispose of the sludge and stone fragments.

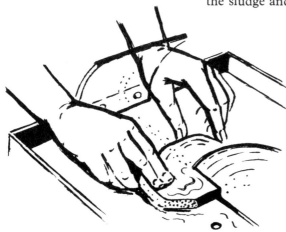

22 Trimming a flat slab on a diamond saw

23 Tumbling action
a Tumbler barrel loaded with stones, grit and water, two-thirds full
b Correct tumbling action, with stones cascading gently
c Excessive speed causes stones to be flung about violently, chipping and fracturing in the process
d Tumbler revolving too slowly, with load slipping along base of the barrel, resulting in flattened stones

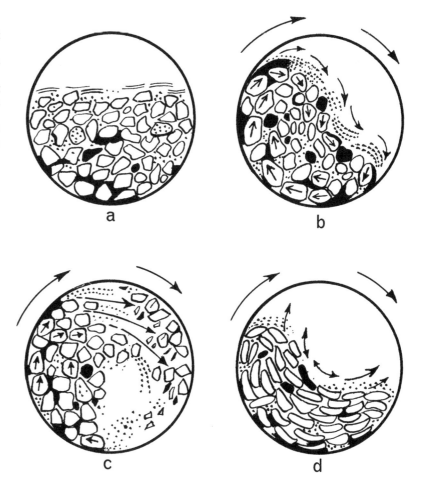

Tumbling process

Polished baroque stones are mass-produced in a revolving drum and because of their relative cheapness are frequently used in popular jewellery. Many people consider the irregular shapes of tumble polished stones to be more attractive than the usual cabochons. Since tumbling is a mechanical process, it requires no particular skill apart from careful supervision of the various stages. As a general rule the operator does not directly influence the resultant shapes, but sometimes stones are pre-shaped by hand on a grinding wheel or trimmed on a diamond saw before tumbling.

24 Smaller stones can assist the tumbling action by grinding into hollows of larger stones

The action of tumbling is comparable to that of sand and surf on sea-shore pebbles. A watertight drum or barrel is loaded about two-thirds full with stones, silicon carbide grit and water. The drum is made to revolve slowly, carrying the stones up the inside of the container and allows them to cascade gently when they reach the angle of fall, sliding and grinding against each other in the process. (Figure 23.) Sharp corners and other imperfections are gradually eliminated by the abrasive action of the grits, used progressively from coarse to fine. A suitable polishing agent is introduced in the final stages. The length of time taken to complete the whole process will vary according to the type of material in the load. A careful selection of stones of similar hardness, avoiding fractured or badly pitted rocks, will produce the best results. Stones of different sizes can be used to advantage at the same time (figure 24) but pieces over 1 in (25 mm) in diameter should not be included as they can easily chip or crack smaller stones during tumbling.

Tumbler construction

Materials:
$\frac{1}{4}$ hp (186·5 watts) electric motor.
Two rollers.
Pulleys and driving belt.
Tumbler drums.

The framework can be of wood or metal and constructed on a firm wooden base with motor in the rear, or the motor can be mounted below the rollers and built into a small bench. (Figures 25 and 26). The roller bearings must allow free running and be bolted securely to the framework. Large and small pulleys will give the correct speed ratio between motor and rollers. A small pulley and belt can connect the two rollers but this is not essential. The length of the rollers and the distance apart will be in proportion to the size of drums being used.

The drums or barrels should be tough and durable, and designed to roll or tumble the stones gently without damage. Suitable thick plastic bottles can be purchased from lapidary suppliers. Should metal drums be used, rubber liners must be fitted and the lids made completely water-tight. Containers can be round or angular, (figure 27), the latter being designed to lift the load prior to rolling.

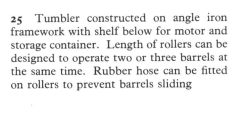

25 Tumbler constructed on angle iron framework with shelf below for motor and storage container. Length of rollers can be designed to operate two or three barrels at the same time. Rubber hose can be fitted on rollers to prevent barrels sliding

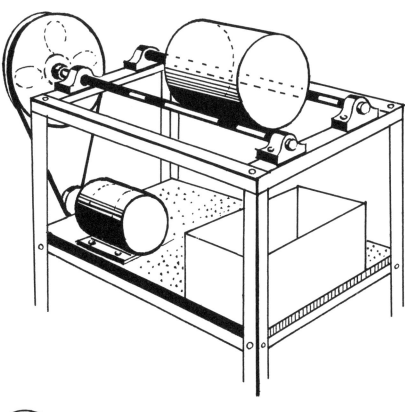

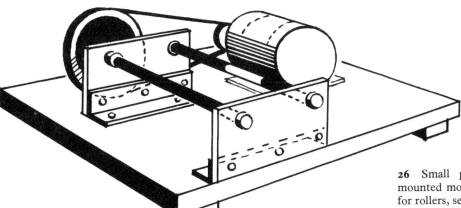

26 Small portable tumbler with rear mounted motor. Metal or wood supports for rollers, secured to base by short lengths of angle iron. Rubber pads screwed beneath base will prevent movement and eliminate vibration

Tumbling phases

Although many experiments have been conducted on the effectiveness of amounts of grit relative to size of load and tumbling period, there are no hard and fast rules for grit and stone ratios. The following quantities are worked out for a 1 gallon (4·5 litres) drum, giving an approximate loading at two-thirds capacity of 6 to 8 lb (3 to 4 kg) of stones. Size, shape and nature of the stones will account for variations of weight and bulk.

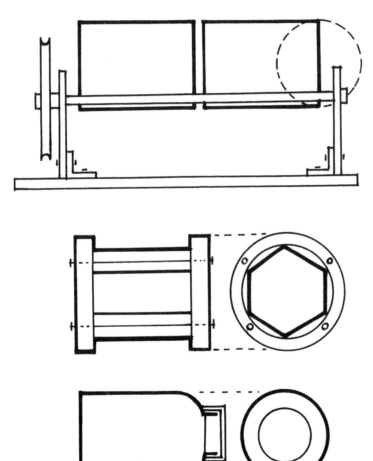

27 Types of tumbler barrels
Top Circular drums
Centre Angular container securely held between circular rings
Bottom Plastic bottle with screw lid. The opening should be large enough to insert the hand for inspection purposes

Phase 1	$\frac{3}{4}$ lb to 1 lb (340 to 454 g) Silicon carbide	80 or 120 grit
Phase 2	$\frac{1}{2}$ lb to $\frac{3}{4}$ lb (227 to 340 g) Silicon carbide	220 or 320 grit
	(optional run).	
Phase 3	$\frac{1}{2}$ lb to $\frac{3}{4}$ lb (227 to 340 g) Silicon carbide	400 or 500 grit
Phase 4	6 oz to 8 oz (170 to 227 g) Polishing agent. Tin oxide, cerium oxide or levigated alumina, with additives	
Phase 5	Final rinse. 1 cup detergent powder and water.	

Some operators omit phase 2 with good results, the reason being that 80 or 120 grit will eventually break down to 220 or 320 grit sizes, given sufficient time.

It is impossible to state a specific period of time for each tumbling phase as this depends on many factors such as, size and shape of barrel, rotation speeds, viscosity of load and continuity of movement. Hardness of the material should also be taken into account. As a rough guide, water-worn pebbles can take from four to seven days in the first grinding. Subsequent grinding can also take four to seven days, and the final polish about two days, followed by a detergent run of 8 to 12 hours. For very rough material, which includes rock hammered into small pieces, the first phase may take two or three weeks of continuous grinding with 80 grit to reduce the stones to reasonable shape. Additional phases, using finer grits can vary between four to seven days, and polishing from two to four days before the detergent run.

Throughout the grinding phases, the tumbler should run continuously day and night. If the tumbler is allowed to remain stationary for any length of time, the sludge and stones settle into a compact mass and until the stones are dislodged from the cement-like mixture it cannot operate efficiently.

Phase 1   Weigh the selected batch of stones and place in the tumbler barrel with the proportionate quantity of 80 grit. The load should occupy two-thirds of the drum capacity. Cover the stones with water, making sure that the lid is water-tight. Rest the drum between the rollers and start the tumbling action, which should be geared to the recommended speed. A steady swishing sound will indicate that the tumbler is functioning correctly. If the sound is intermittent, the stones are sliding on the side of the drum and this may be caused by too slow rotation or insufficient stones in the load.

Inspect the contents of the tumbler every 24 hours to check on the progress and eliminate any gas which may have formed. This is more likely to occur when unlined metal containers are used, which contributes to a build-up of hydrogen gas. The addition of a tablespoonful of baking soda to the load will help to prevent this.

During a long run of two or three weeks, a renewal of 80 grit will be necessary due to the gradual breakdown of the effective grit size. The grinding action on the stones produces an accumulation of waste which combines with the grit to form a thick sludge. If this becomes too thick the stones will not move freely and more water should be added.

When most of the stones are smooth and free from irregularities, empty the contents of the tumbler into a coarse sieve and rinse thoroughly. The thick sludge must not be disposed of in the domestic drainage system or a blockage will certainly occur. It is preferable to disperse the sludge into the ground but if this is not possible, contain it in a strong polythene bag and drain off all surplus water before placing in the dustbin.

Phase 2 or 3 The stones and tumbler barrel must be thoroughly cleaned between each phase. Replace the stones and re-charge the barrel with the appropriate grit and water. The bulk of the stones will have been reduced by about 10 or 15 per cent during the rough grinding and the load level must be made up with filler such as smooth quartz pebbles. Continue tumbling, with regular inspections, until the stones acquire a smooth refined surface.

Phase 4 Rinse the stones and barrel repeatedly, paying attention to the lid and any sealing rings, until every trace of grit has been removed. Ideally, a separate barrel should be kept solely for polishing but if this is not practical, the utmost care must be taken to avoid contaminating the polish with grit particles.

Place the stones in the tumbler very gently to avoid chipping, cover with water and add the polishing agent. Polishing aids, or additives, can be included at this stage to soften the impact of the stones and make up the load level. Among the many additives used are small pieces of felt, scraps of sole-leather, vermiculite and plastic granules. Continue polishing until a satisfactory result has been achieved.

Phase 5 Clean out the barrel once more and replace the stones in a mixture of clean water and detergent powder for the final run.

Tumbler speeds

Diameter of drum	Recommended speeds
6 in (152 mm)	35 to 50 rpm
8 in (203 mm)	30 to 45 rpm
10 in (254 mm)	25 to 40 rpm
12 in (305 mm)	20 to 30 rpm

The slower speeds are recommended for angular drums which have a more pronounced tumbling action. Also, for round drums when using a batch of brittle or very soft stones. It may be necessary to off-set slow running by allowing extra tumbling time.

Cutting a cabochon

The beauty of a stone is revealed by the way in which it is cut and polished. Stones depending upon light refraction to express their character, such as diamonds, emeralds, sapphires and other transparent stones, are usually faceted. The mathematical arrangement of planes around the surface of the stone is carried out by mechanical means, using a faceting attachment on a lapidary machine.

Opaque or translucent stones, which includes the largest proportion of those found in Britain, are more suitable for polishing in any of the different cabochon shapes. Cutting an oval cabochon, as outlined in this chapter, is a good introduction to the basic skill of the lapidary craft.

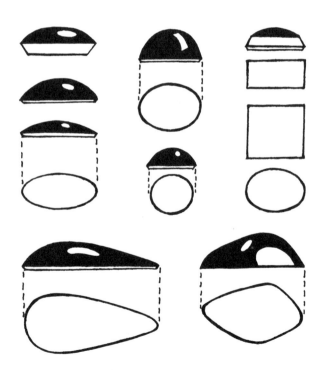

28 Cabochon shapes

Choosing a shape

The shape of a cabochon may be determined by such things as the nature of the material, a particular jewellery setting, or the outcome of a creative exercise. Rough stone which is bought, slabbed and trimmed, from lapidary suppliers must be carefully considered in order to retain the essential features. With a few modifications, beach pebbles often suggest interesting shapes for a more creative approach. The height of a cabochon can range from a slightly raised surface to a high dome. (Figure 28.)

Selecting and marking out the rough stone

Having obtained a stone of sufficient thickness for shaping a cabochon dome, examine it carefully under a good light to check for possible flaws. A small magnifying lens is useful for this purpose. Shallow imperfections on the surface will probably grind away but stones with deep cracks or internal fractures should be discarded.

After deciding which surface will exploit the qualities of the stone to best advantage for the cabochon dome, the base oval is then marked out on the opposite side. This is a simple matter when using trimmed stones with two flat surfaces, but in the case of unslabbed rough or beach pebbles it will be necessary to grind a flat surface in order to establish a suitable base. The shape should be drawn on the stone with a pointed piece of aluminium so that the mark will not wash off during the cutting process. An even shape can more easily be obtained if a template is used which has holes punched out in a variety of cabochon sizes. (Figure 29).

29 Using a pointed piece of aluminium wire to mark out cabochon shape. Templates are manufactured in stiff plastic

Cutting the basic shape

Depending on the hardness of the stone, the first grinding is done on a coarse or medium wheel, 60 or 120 grit, turning at a little below 3000 rpm. Beach pebbles or uneven pieces of rock can be roughly shaped on the 60 grit, followed by refinements on the 120 grit. The front edge of the wheel is the cutting surface, the side should only be used occasionally to smooth away any slight imperfections on flat surfaces and never for grinding. (Figure 30.)

Make sure the wheel is in contact with water, either from a trough below or by overhead drip arrangement, taking care not to soak the wheel. Never allow water to be in contact with the wheel when it is stationary. This upsets the balance of the wheel and weakens the bonding, causing crumbling or uneven wear during subsequent grinding. A small wad of newspaper, rubber strip or cloth, attached to the splash guard and almost touching the wheel, will protect the operator from spray by directing excess water back on to the wheel.

Method Holding the stone firmly, with the base oval uppermost, press it against the revolving wheel just below halfway. (Figure 31.) Avoid excessive pressure and do not jab the stone into the wheel or attempt to cut large chunks of rock as this causes severe grooving of the grinding surface. Keep the stone moving, using the whole width of the wheel to prevent uneven wear. (Figure 32.) Continue grinding until the oval shape has been formed, stopping frequently to wash away the sludge which accumulates on the edge of the stone. A convenient bowl of water can be used for this purpose, or pressure on a sponge placed in the water tray.

To tidy up the base shape and to avoid crumbling at the edge, a very fine bevel is cut on the perimeter of the oval. This is done by holding the stone at an angle to the side of the wheel and making a quick sweep around the edge. (Figure 33.) With the formation of the cabochon base, the first stage is now complete and the stone ready for mounting on a dopstick for further cutting.

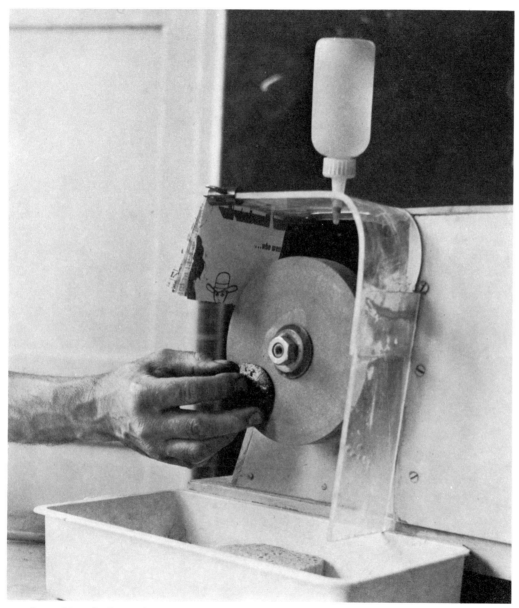

30 Smoothing the base of the stone on the side of the wheel
to remove saw marks and results of rough grinding

31 Grinding the oval base of the cabochon. This has been marked
out from a template with an aluminium pencil

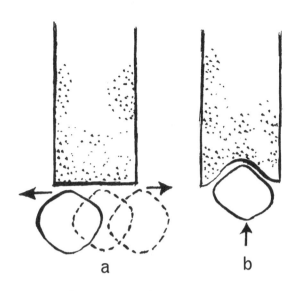

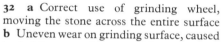

32 a Correct use of grinding wheel, moving the stone across the entire surface
b Uneven wear on grinding surface, caused by holding stone in one position
c Complete misuse of the wheel. Grinding into side of wheel must be avoided

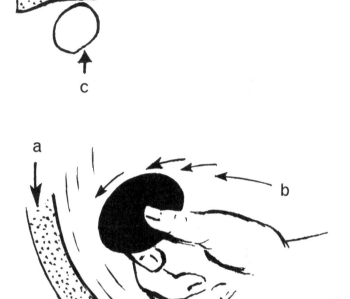

33 Cutting a fine bevel on the perimeter of the stone at the base, using a quick sweeping movement
a Direction of grinding wheel
b Direction of stone sweeping across the side of the wheel
c Angle of stone to the side of the wheel, making required bevel

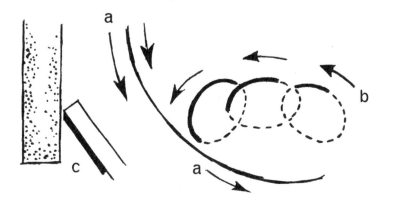

65

Dopping the stone

With a little experience, larger stones can be held and worked quite successfully in the fingers. It is advisable for beginners, and essential when cutting stones for small settings, to mount the stone on a dopstick which allows greater freedom in handling. A carefully dopped stone will remain in position throughout every stage of grinding and polishing, so it is important to adopt a methodical approach.

Dopsticks can be made from anything which will perform the function of a short narrow handle. Pencils, dowelling, thin metal tubing, or even a six inch nail with a flat head, are all suitable. The use of round wooden dowelling is perhaps the best of these as it can easily be cut into lengths, of approximately six inches, and the diameter can be selected to suit the size of the stone.

One of the most satisfactory forms of adhesive for mounting the stone on the dopstick is dopping wax. This can be bought ready-made in sticks from lapidary suppliers or you can make it up yourself.

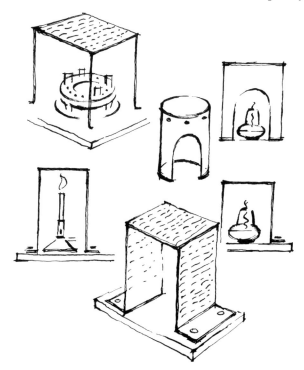

34 Supports used for metal plate used for melting dopping wax and heating stones. Simple wire mesh frame can be constructed, or a hole cut into a can to provide access for a small spirit lamp

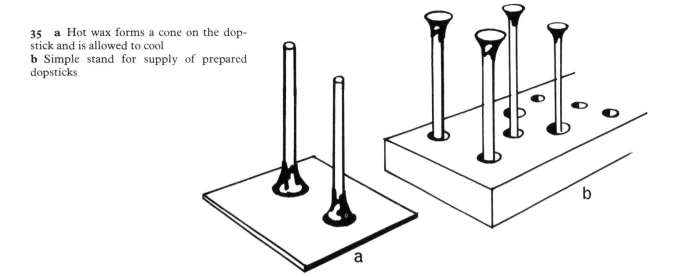

35 a Hot wax forms a cone on the dop-stick and is allowed to cool
b Simple stand for supply of prepared dopsticks

The ingredients are sealing wax and shellac, melted with a little beeswax to make the mixture more pliable and lower the melting point. Take care not to overheat and burn.

To prepare the dopsticks, place the tin containing the wax on a metal plate heated over a gasring, bunsen burner or spirit lamp. (Figure 34.) Dip the end of the dowel into the liquid wax to a depth of about half an inch, turning the stick slowly until it becomes evenly covered with wax. Remove quickly and place upright, waxed end downwards, on a smooth cool surface. This allows the wax to settle slowly to form an even cone at the end of the stick. (Figure 35a.) When the wax is cool the dopstick is ready for use. Prepare several dopsticks of different dimensions at the same time so that you have a selection for any size of stone. A block of wood drilled with holes will make a convenient stand for your supply of dopsticks. (Figure 35b.)

When ready for fixing the stone to the dopstick, place the stone on the hot plate, base uppermost. The stone must be hot enough to make a bond with the dopping wax, but care must be taken not to overheat and crack the stone. Opals and other sensitive stones can be heated slowly on a tray of sand to avoid direct contact with the hot plate.

Select one of the prepared dopsticks and soften the wax over a

flame. (Figure 36.) Press the wax on to the warm stone and lift clear of the hot plate. (Figure 37.) Holding the stick and stone upright, proceed to centre the stone and mould the wax onto it with finger and thumb, making a firm well-supported platform. (Figure 38.) The wax must be allowed to cool and thoroughly harden before beginning to grind the stone. Should the stone become detached from the dopstick for any reason, it is a simple matter to repeat the dopping process.

Cutting the cabochon dome

Continue to use the 120 grit wheel, running at the cutting speed of 3000 rpm and apply water coolant. Hold the dopstick as shown, (Figure 39), and press the stone firmly against the abrasive surface.

36 Softening the dopping wax

37 a Melted wax being pressed on to heated stone
b Wax makes a bond with the stone which is then lifted clear of the hot plate

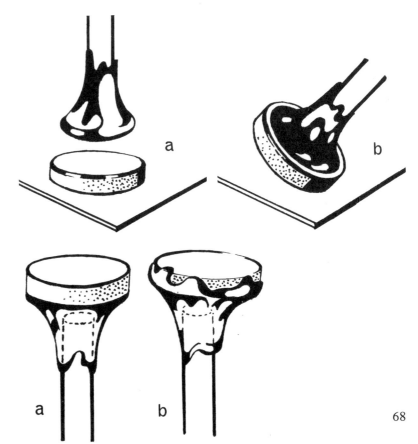

38 a Correctly dopped stone, evenly supported on the wax. The stone does not come into contact with the end of the dowel
b Badly dopped stone. Off centre, making it difficult to cut a symmetrical cabochon. Wax should not spread over stone, this can lead to unpolished areas

39 Shaping the cabochon dome. Note position of the hands holding dopstick and point of contact between wheel and stone, which should be a little below half way. The dopstick is manipulated with the right hand, rocking or rotating as required

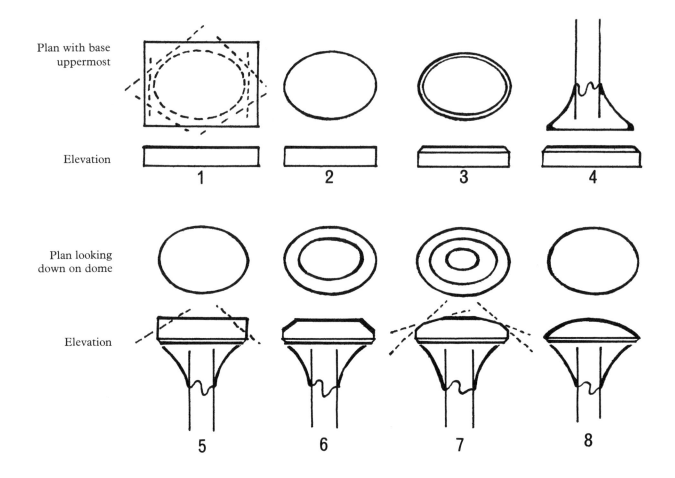

Plan with base uppermost

Elevation

1 2 3 4

Plan looking down on dome

Elevation

5 6 7 8

40a Progressive stages in cutting a cabochon. Use of flat slabs, trimmed to workable sizes

Cutting the oval base **1** Oval shape marked out on the stone. Corners can be trimmed off with a diamond saw or ground away on the wheel **2** Shape ground close to the line marked with aluminium pencil **3** Fine bevel cut on the base. This prevents edge crumbling away during grinding **4** Base now ready for dopstick

Shaping the dome **5** Stone supported on dopstick. Dotted lines show direction of first cuts **6** Angle of first cut, almost down to the base **7** Second cut, with change of angles **8** Cabochon dome shaped after subsequent cuts and elimination of points and facets

70

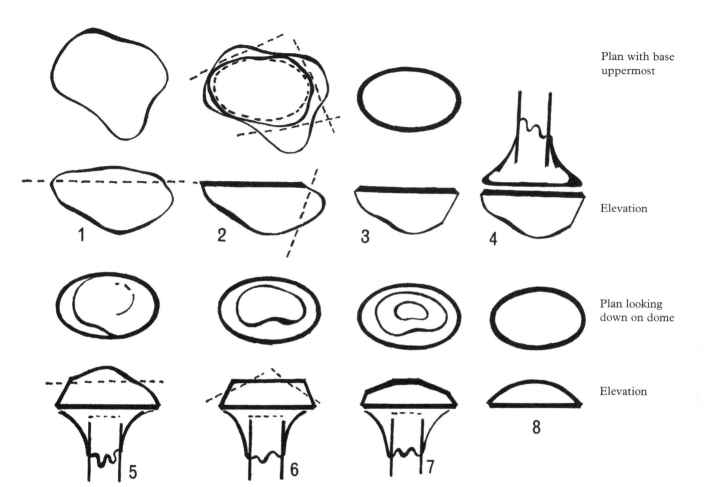

Plan with base uppermost

Elevation

Plan looking down on dome

Elevation

40b Progressive stages in cutting a cabochon. Procedure with irregular-shaped pebbles or uneven gemstone rough

Cutting the base **1** Dotted line shows extent of first grinding to form suitable base **2** Flat face established. Dotted lines show oval base marked out and direction of cuts to remove bumps **3** Base shaped to the oval mark. No other portion of the stone should now be visible beyond the base line. Cut a fine bevel on the perimeter **4** Base now ready for fixing to dopstick
Shaping the dome **5** Dotted line shows first area to be removed **6** and **7** Subsequent cutting with changing angles **8** Completed cabochon shape, ready for sanding phases

71

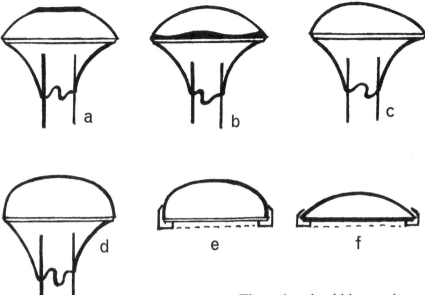

41 Common faults in shaping a cabochon dome
a Flat top to dome
b Wavy edge near the base
c Stone not symmetrical. May be due to badly centred dopping
d Sides of the dome too vertical
e Vertical sides unsuitable for setting
f Correctly shaped cabochon, allowing good wrapover for bezel setting

The action should be steady and deliberate as any hesitancy when contacting the wheel may chip the stone. Turn the stick slowly, using a sweeping movement upwards and across the front of the wheel, gradually cutting a bevel almost to the base of the stone. (Figures 40a and b). Change the angle of the dopstick and cut a second bevel. (Figures 40a and b.) Wash the stone frequently as cutting proceeds. By gently rotating and rocking the end of the dopstick with the right hand and turning it with the left, it is a simple matter to round off the cabochon dome. (Figures 40a and b.)

Wash and dry the stone and inspect carefully under a good light. Check the shape for symmetry and ensure that the surface is smooth and free from points or facets before proceeding to the finer grinding wheel. Common faults at this stage are illustrated in figure 41.

Final grinding

The final shaping is done on the 220 grit wheel turning at the same cutting speed as before. Add water coolant.

At this stage the stone must be kept moving continuously by turning, rocking and rotating the dopstick. Failure to do this will result in a series of tiny facets which have to be removed before going on to the next phase. Gradually easing up on the pressure, continue this movement until all the abrasive marks made by the 120 grit wheel have been smoothed away.

Dry the stone and carry out further inspection under a light. Slight imperfections can also be detected by running the fingertips lightly over the surface of the stone. When satisfied that the stone is quite smooth and of pleasing shape from all aspects, proceed to the sanding phases.

Sanding with abrasive grits

The sanding process described here is carried out on a horizontal machine, using leather discs and loose abrasive grits. Selection of grit sizes is a matter of experience and preference. Satisfactory results are obtained using 220, 320 and 500 grades of silicon carbide grits, progressively from coarse to fine, on separate leather discs. As a general rule, this sequence of grit sizes will produce good results but for some stones finer grades of grit may be used, omitting the 320 grade.

The importance of keeping the different grades of grit powders entirely separate cannot be over-stressed. It is recommended that the leather discs be stored in individual polythene bags to prevent contamination by other grits or dirt and dust. Careful storage and a methodical working procedure should be strictly observed. Washing the hands, stone and equipment between each sanding phase is essential. Should even a few grains of coarser grit get on to a disc intended for use with a finer grade of grit, it would scratch the stone and make it impossible to continue with the finer sanding. The leather disc would have to be thoroughly scrubbed to remove all traces of grit.

In order to determine the running speed for the sanding process, various factors must be taken into consideration. If the wheel is revolving too quickly, the loose grit powders are flung off before they can be used. The type of stone being polished must be considered since a harder stone requires a faster speed for sanding to be effective. A softer stone, or one which is easily affected by heat, requires a slower sanding speed. The highest speed for sanding should not be more than 1425 rpm and it can be geared down to approximately 800 rpm if necessary. A little experimentation will

42 Sanding on horizontal lapping disc, and application of grit from a squeezy bottle

soon prove to the operator which is the most suitable speed for his purpose.

Commence with the leather disc intended for the 220 grit, applying the grit and water from a plastic squeezy bottle as the disc revolves. (Figure 42.) Press the stone firmly to the disc, holding the dopstick with the fingers low down near to the stone. Using a circular motion, rock and turn the dopstick. Apply light to moderate pressure, increasing on the backward movement against the direction of the wheel. (Figure 43.) Keep the stone moving, sanding the whole surface, and apply more grit when needed. The abrasive bite of the grit can be heard when the disc is functioning correctly. Pay particular attention to the rim of the stone, close to the base, as this is often neglected in the early stages.

There is no fixed time limit for each sanding phase. The best results are achieved by continuing until all marks from the previous stages have been removed. Check progress frequently, and continue working on the 220 grit disc until the surface of the stone shows an even dull lustre. Any irregularity of surface will be clearly revealed at this stage, which may necessitate a return to the 220 grinding wheel.

When satisfied that the stone is quite smooth, progress from the 220 grit through the 320 and 500 grit stages. Carry out the same procedure, using a different disc for each grade of grit. Wash hands and stone carefully between each phase, and return discs and grits to their appropriate storage compartments. Before proceeding to the final polishing stage, make sure that all traces of abrasive grit are removed from the working area. Care must be taken not to put the stone down on a gritty surface, and it is useful to have a clean soft tissue on which to place the stone.

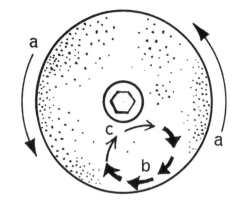

43 Fluctuating pressure on stone during sanding. The whole operation to be carried out in a continuous circular motion
a Direction of wheel
b Dark arrows. Pressure increases against direction of revolving disc
c Light arrows. Indicate easing up on pressure

Final polishing

Adjust the driving belt to turn the disc at a slower speed, approximately 750 rpm. Attach the hard felt polishing disc, or a disc of soft leather which is preferable for heat-sensitive stones. Either tin oxide or cerium oxide, mixed with water, can be used as the polishing agent. A separate disc must be kept for each type of polish. A thin solution of polish, mixed in a shallow dish, is applied with a soft brush across the revolving wheel, (figure 44), or the mixture can be applied from a squeezy bottle.

Using moderate pressure, move the dopstick as before and continue until the stone acquires a high gloss. If the disc is allowed to become too dry, frictional heat can crack the stone or burn the surface, causing a permanent dull patch. To avoid overheating, the stone should be rinsed frequently in a bowl of clean water. When every part of the stone is evenly polished, it can be removed from the dopstick.

Removing stone from dopstick

Hold the dopstick over a small flame, turning it slowly, until the wax begins to melt. Take hold of the stone with a cloth and, with a quick twist, remove the stone from the wax. The stone should come away cleanly but any remaining wax can be cleaned off with methylated spirit.

An alternative method is to place the dopstick in the freezing compartment of a refrigerator for a few minutes. The stone can then be removed cleanly from the dopstick.

Alternative sanding methods

Horizontal cast iron laps are used for sanding thin slabs or smooth flat surfaces. Loose abrasive grit is applied as before, grading from coarse to fine, and the slab is held firmly on the revolving disc. Moderate pressure should be used, taking care not to tilt the stone to ensure a perfectly flat face. If the slab is too thin to hold comfortably, it can be fixed to a block of wood with gum solution. Wash the lap and stone thoroughly between changes of grit. Similar methods can be employed when using loose grits on discs of copper, perspex and hard wood.

Variations in speeds are necessary when working with hard surfaced laps. Leather discs, and to some extent copper and perspex, retain the grits which become embedded in the surface. Cast iron laps, running at similar speeds, have a tendency to scatter the grits. Experience is the best guide to the most suitable running speeds.

A more expensive method of sanding involves the use of copper discs impregnated with diamond powder or the application of diamond paste. These are effectively used in faceting the harder gemstones, but not essential for general lapidary purposes.

Another satisfactory sanding method uses graded silicon carbide paper, or cloth, discs, gummed to a resilient backing on a firm support. (Figure 45.) These can be used on both vertical and horizontal machines, and should turn at the motor speed of 1425 rpm. The sanding progression need only involve two grades, 220 and 400, prior to the polishing stage. The discs can be used wet or dry but application of water from a squeezy bottle is recommended to avoid overheating the stone during sanding. For individual use, this

44 Final polishing phase, using a horizontal felt wheel. The polishing agent is being applied with a soft brush. The felt polishing wheel can also be used in a vertical position

method of sanding is speedier than using loose grits but less economical, as the paper discs have to be renewed frequently. Sanding on a horizontal lap with loose abrasives has the added advantage of being accessible to more than one person at the same time and this is an important consideration when working with groups of students.

45 Alternative method of sanding, using a vertical disc of abrasive cloth or paper

Imported rocks

In addition to the standard gemstone minerals which are classified as precious or semi-precious, many lesser known varieties are now accepted in fashionable jewellery for beauty of pattern and colour regardless of rarity or permanence.

Large quantities of rocks and minerals are imported into this country for jewellery purposes and an extensive range of rough material, which is graded according to quality and sold by the pound, ounce or carat, is now available to the lapidary and collector. The cheapest method of obtaining gemstone rough is to purchase large unslabbed pieces and then cut them to size with a diamond saw. If the stone has been hammered into rough pieces, it should be examined carefully for cracks and flaws before purchase. Thin slabs of rough are slightly more expensive and usually sold by the square inch. For an additional fee, some dealers will trim the slabs into workable sizes as required.

The following list will serve as a guide to some of the popular stones suitable for cabochons and tumbling, or the formation of an inexpensive collection. A more comprehensive range of material available is listed in dealers' catalogues.

Green varieties

Aventurine
> Crystalline quartz. Hardness: 7. Translucent. Light to deep green. Compact material with minute crystals of mica producing a glittering effect through the stone. *Locations :* Brazil, India.

Amazonite
> Microcline feldspar. Hardness: 6. Opaque to translucent. Deep green to blue green, pale turquoise. With schiller effect. *Locations :* America, Canada.

Bloodstone (Heliotrope)
> Cryptocrystalline quartz. Hardness: 7. Opaque. Dark green chalcedony, spotted with red. *Location :* India.

Chrysoprase
> Cryptocrystalline quartz. Hardness: 7. Translucent. Bright green chalcedony. *Locations :* America, Brazil, Australia.

Malachite
Copper carbonate. Hardness: 3–4. Opaque. Deep to pale green. Variegated green ribbon and circular banding. *Locations :* Africa, USSR, America.

Blue varieties

Sodalite
Sodium-aluminium silicate. Hardness: 5–6. Translucent. Deep to paler blue, also streaked with white or grey. *Locations :* Canada, India, South America.

Lapis Lazuli
Lazurite and calcite. Hardness: 5. Opaque. Ultramarine blue, speckled with gold-coloured inclusions of pyrites. Poorer quality streaked with white or grey. *Locations :* Afghanistan, USSR, USA, Pakistan, South America.

Amethyst
Crystalline quartz. Hardness: 7. Transparent and semi-transparent. Deep purple, good quality transparent for faceting. Paler purple. Massive. Semi-transparent with colour zoning. *Locations :* Mexico, Brazil, USA, USSR, Australia.

Red, brown, yellow varieties

Carnelian
Cryptocrystalline quartz. Hardness: 7. Semi-transparent. Pale orange to deep red chalcedony. Compact. *Locations :* Widely distributed.

Tigereye
Quartz replacement of asbestos. Hardness: 7. Opaque. Golden brown, yellow-green, blue, red. Silky fibres giving chatoyance. *Locations :* South Africa.

Jasper
Quartz. Hardness: 6–7. Opaque. Chalcedony with coloured impurities. Variety of colour and pattern. Red to brownish colours predominant. *Locations :* Widely distributed.

Rose quartz
Crystalline. Hardness: 7. Translucent. Pink with cloudy appearance. Often has internal fractures, not detrimental to cutting and polishing. *Location :* Brazil.

Rhodonite

> Manganese silicate. Hardness: 5–6. Opaque. Pale pink to red, veined with black or yellow. Best quality finely grained and compact. *Locations:* USA, Australia, Canada.

Rhodochrosite

> Manganese carbonate. Hardness: 3–4. Opaque. Pink to deep red, with satin sheen. Banding of pink and red tints, streaked with white. *Locations:* USA, South America.

Agate varieties   Cryptocrystalline quartz. Hardness: 7.

The following are selected from numerous varieties:

Banded, fortification and orbicular agates. Colours ranging from milky white to pale blue chalcedony, with black, red, brown, yellow or green in bands of contrasting tones.

Moss agate: clear translucent chalcedony with moss or fern-like inclusions. Usually green but blue and red varieties are obtainable.

Plume and flame agate: translucent. Coloured inclusions resembling feathers or smoke.

Scenic agate: opaque to translucent. Inclusions suggesting mountains, forests, lakes.

Lace agate: opaque. Finely banded, with intricate lace patterns.

> *Locations:* agates are imported from world-wide sources. Beautiful specimens from Australia, India, Africa, Mexico, USA, Brazil. Idar Oberstein, Germany, is a renowned agate centre, where large amounts of clear agate is imported and artificially stained for re-distribution in world markets.

Other varieties

Petrified wood   Remains of ancient forests preserved by mineral replacement of wood structure. Extensive range of colour and pattern. Composition can have the qualities of agate, jasper or opal. *Locations:* America, Australia.

Obsidian   Volcanic glass. Amorphous. Hardness: 5. Translucent. Intense black to reddish brown. Can be striped or smoky. Opaque black variety, spotted with star-like inclusions of white or grey, known as *snowflake obsidian*. Transparent smoky brown obsidian, found in small nodules, known as *apache tears*. *Locations:* America, USSR.

Rutilated quartz Crystalline. Hardness: 7. Transparent. Clear quartz with inclusions of golden rutile needles. Quartz can be colourless, smoky yellow or a delicate wine colour. *Locations:* South America, Canada, USA.

Tourmaline in quartz Crystalline. Hardness: 7. Transparent. Clear quartz with needle-like inclusions of black tourmaline. *Locations:* South America.

Lapidary as a school craft

In the following activities suggested for schools and colleges, the emphasis is on the obvious link between lapidary and jewellery as an integrated course of study, enabling students to participate in each creative stage. Projects stimulated by collecting and polishing stones can be geared to age groups and environment.

Suggestions for a combined lapidary and jewellery course

Design and construction of suitable machines from manufactured components.

Study of lapidary processes, nature and function of abrasive and polishing materials.

Cutting and polishing stones available from British and imported sources which are suitable for setting in a variety of ways.

a Cabochons for rings, pendants and brooches, using claw and bezel settings.

b Utilising shapes suggested by pebbles or modifications of crystal forms, giving opportunities for more creative settings and exploitation of the qualities of the stone.

c Sawing or grinding thin slabs or flat sections. Experiments with contrasting polished and unpolished areas as a basis for imaginative settings.

d Use of irregular shaped tumbled stones for setting in rings, bracelets and necklaces, or sliced into matching pairs for cuff-links and earrings.

e Jewellery forms combining polished stones and other materials with contrasting or harmonious features, such as perspex or wood with pleasing grain patterns. Use of epoxy resin as an alternative method of setting.

f Use of small pebbles or stone fragments closely set in resin or plaster, the surface ground and polished in the usual way, used for ornamental and jewellery purposes. Matching pairs can be made by using a diamond saw to slice through blocks containing pebbles.

Additional group or individual activities

Mosaics, using round or flat pebbles polished by machine or hand methods. Intarsia or inlaid pictures, using thin polished slabs of multi-coloured, textured stones, suitable for wall decorations, trays or small tables.

Analysis of pattern. Study of polished rock and fossil sections as a basis for drawing, painting or fabric printing.

Carving and polishing techniques with soft stone, using drills and mops in a flexible drive.

Environment studies

Research into polished building stone in the locality. Survey of buildings with polished facing stone, columns or ornament. Type of stone used.

Geological and geographical origins. Visits to quarries and stone polishing firms. Studies of colour and pattern. Drawings and photographs with local or historical interest.

Use of polished ornamental stone inside churches, museums and country houses. The following features show a prolific use of polished stone:

Sculpture and ornament. Commemorative plaques. Columns, floors, staircases, fire places. Chandeliers of faceted rock crystal. Table surfaces, vases.

Materials frequently used include marbles, granites, feldspars, serpentine, fossil limestones, onyx, fluorspar (variety Blue John).

46 Silver pendant with cabochon of polished porphyry

47 Silver pendant with polished agate section. Features of stones used as a basis for creative setting

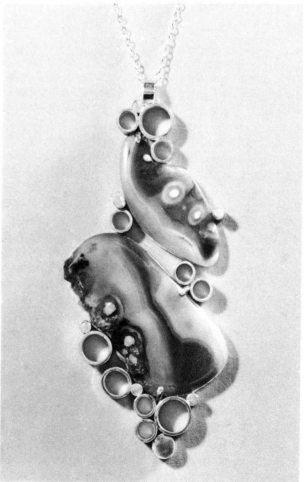

Lapidary societies in Great Britain

The Sutherland Rockhounds, Dornoch, Sutherland.
The Scottish Mineral and Lapidary Club, Edinburgh.
West of Scotland Mineral and Lapidary Society, Glasgow.
Kingston Lapidary Society, Hull, Yorkshire.
The North West Lapidary Society, Cheshire.
The Danum Lapidary Society, Doncaster, Yorkshire.
The Leeds Lapidary Society, Leeds, Yorkshire.
Wessex Lapidary Society, Winchester, Hampshire.
Essex Rock and Mineral Society, Romford, Essex.
Teesside Lapidary Society, Middlesborough, Teesside.

Suppliers of lapidary equipment

Most of these firms are able to supply all the requirements for
amateur lapidary, including machines, wheels and grits, and rough
stone for polishing.
Gemrocks Limited, Halton House, 20/3 Holborn, London, EC1.
Kernowcraft Rocks and Gems, 68 Highertown, Truro, Cornwall.
M. L. Beach, FGA, 41 Church Street, Twickenham, Middlesex.
P.M.R. Lapidary Equipment and Supplies, Smithy House, Atholl
   Road, Pitlochry, Perthshire.
Hirsh Jacobson Merchandising Co. Ltd, 29 Ludgate Hill, London,
   EC4.
Minerals and Gemstones (Penzance), Trewellard Road, Pendeen,
   Penzance, Cornwall.
Wessex Gems and Crafts Ltd, Gemini, Lanham Lane, Winchester,
   Hampshire.
Fisher Gems and Minerals, 43 Hazelwood Road, Northampton.
Kenneth Parkinson, FGA, 11 Fitzroy Street, Hull, Yorkshire.
Gemstones, 35 Princes Avenue, Hull, Yorkshire.
Ammonite Limited, Llandow Industrial Estate, Cowbridge,
   Glamorgan.
Whithear Lapidary Co., 35 Ballards Lane, London, N3.
Sutherland Gem Cutters, Achmelvich by Lairg, Scotland.
Baines, Orr & Co. (Pty) Ltd, 3 Felixstowe Road, London, NW10.

Index

FURTHER READING

Fossils
F. H. T. Rhodes, H. S. Zim, P. R.
    Shaffer
Paul Hamlyn 1965

Rocks and Minerals
H. S. Zim, P. R. Shaffer
Paul Hamlyn 1965

Minerals and Rocks in Colour
J. F. Kirkaldy
Blandford Press 1963

Collecting Rocks and Fossils
J. B. Delair
B. T. Batsford 1966

The Pebbles on the Beach
C. Ellis
Faber and Faber 1957

A New Geology
M. Bradshaw
The English Universities Press 1968

Gem Cutting
J. Sinkankas
D. Van Nostrand Co. U.S.A. 1962

Jewels
P. J. Fisher
B. T. Batsford 1965

Practical Gemmology
R. Webster
N.A.G. Press 1957